HAKEEM OLAJUWON

THE ACHIEVERS

HAKEEM OLAJUWON
tower of power

George R. Rekela

Lerner Publications Company ▪ Minneapolis

Information in this book came from the author's interview with Hakeem
Olajuwon, as well as from the following sources: *The Sporting News,
Basketball Digest, People, Street and Smith's Pro Basketball, Ebony,
Houston Chronicle, Houston Rockets Media Guide, New York Times, USA
Today, University of Houston Basketball Media Guide, The Associated
Press, Sports Illustrated*, and *Jet.*

This book is available in two editions:
Library binding by Lerner Publications Company
Soft cover by First Avenue Editions
241 First Avenue North, Minneapolis, Minnesota 55401

LIBRARY OF CONGRESS CATALOGING-IN-PUBLICATION DATA

Rekela, George R., 1943-
    Hakeem Olajuwon : tower of power / George R. Rekela.
        p.   cm. — (The Achievers)
    Summary: Chronicles the career of the NBA center from
his journey from Nigeria to the University of Houston through
his success in professional basketball.
    ISBN 0-8225-0518-5 (lib. bdg.) ISBN 0-8225-9637-7 (pbk.)
    1. Olajuwon, Hakeem, 1963-   —Juvenile literature.
2. Basketball players—United States—Biography—Juve-
nile literature. [1. Olajuwon, Hakeem, 1963-   . 2. Basketball players. 3. Blacks—Nigeria—Biography.]   I. Title.
II. Series.
GV884.O43R45   1993
796.323'092—dc20
[B]   92-38905
                                                                 CIP
                                                                  AC

Manufactured in the United States of America

International Standard Book Number: 0-8225-0518-5 (lib. bdg.)
International Standard Book Number: 0-8225-9637-7 (pbk.)
Library of Congress Catalog Card Number: 92-38905

1   2   3   4   5   6   98   97   96   95   94   93

Contents

1
The Quadruple-Double

The Houston Rockets raced down the floor before 15,088 screaming fans at the arena Texans call "The Summit." Leading the fast break against the Milwaukee Bucks was the Rockets' 7-foot center. As he soared toward the basket, Hakeem Olajuwon (ah-KEEM oh-LA-joo-wan) brushed aside a Milwaukee defender. Having timed his jump perfectly, Olajuwon jammed the ball through the rim.

Basketball fans in Houston were accustomed to seeing Olajuwon put on a show for them. After all, they had watched him for nearly 10 years, since he was a student-athlete at the nearby University of Houston. Now he played for Houston's National Basketball Association (NBA) team, the Rockets. Fans expected him to dominate games—blocking shots, pulling down rebounds, stealing passes, and slamming dunks through the hoop. Seldom did

Hakeem disappoint them. But on this night, March 29, 1990, he would outdo himself.

The NBA keeps track of each player's field goals, free throws, rebounds, blocked shots, steals, turnovers, fouls, and a host of other statistics. Hakeem usually paid little attention to his numbers. "I'm not a player who plays for statistics," he would say after the game. "I play to win. That's what's important to me."

Even so, Rockets fans noticed in the second half that Hakeem was nearing double figures (10 or more for the game) in four categories: points, rebounds, shots blocked, and assists. (An assist is a pass that leads directly to a teammate scoring.) He was approaching what is known in the NBA as a "quadruple-double." During the 1980s, triple-doubles became common for versatile NBA superstars like Magic Johnson, Michael Jordan, and Larry Bird. Hakeem already had six of his own triple-doubles. Quadruple-doubles are much harder to attain. Only two players had accomplished the feat before.

With four minutes to play in the final quarter, Olajuwon had already reached double figures in rebounds, shots blocked, and points scored. He had eight assists, and needed two more to reach double figures. Even though the Rockets held a commanding lead, coach Don Chaney left his star center in the game. As long as Hakeem was so close to a quadruple-double, Chaney wanted to see him get it.

"Hakeem is a competitor all the way," Chaney said. "Before I coached the Rockets, I always respected his game, and now I respect it even more. He plays hard all the time, and that's unusual for a superstar."

Olajuwon passed the ball to teammate Vernon Maxwell, who stepped beyond the three-point line and fired the ball toward the basket. The shot hit nothing but net, giving Hakeem his ninth assist. A minute later, Lewis Lloyd worked his way free and took a pass from Olajuwon. He scored on a short jump shot, and Hakeem had his quadruple-double. He had 18 points, 16 rebounds, 11 blocked shots, and 10 assists.

Hakeem can do just about anything on the basketball court. He excels at dunking, shooting, passing, blocking shots, and stealing the ball from opponents.

Alvin Robertson (left) was one of only two players to earn a quadruple-double before Hakeem accomplished his in 1990. The other player to get a quadruple-double was Hall of Famer Nate Thurmond.

When Chaney sent in a substitute, Olajuwon walked to the bench and was treated to a standing ovation from the appreciative Texas fans.

After the game, one of Hakeem's well-wishers was Milwaukee Bucks guard Alvin Robertson, who had accomplished the most recent NBA quadruple-double. Robertson did it in 1986 when he was playing for the San Antonio Spurs.

Even before his quadruple-double, Olajuwon had taken his place as one of the NBA's best players. His accomplishments were truly amazing, especially considering he never played basketball until he was 15 years old.

2

Coming to America

Hakeem wasn't like Larry Bird, who dribbled a rubber basketball when he was four, or Michael Jordan, who practiced at an 8-foot basket when he was five. Instead, Hakeem grew up playing soccer and team handball in his homeland of Nigeria, a nation on the African continent.

A sensitive and shy youngster, Hakeem felt awkward among his playmates. "It seemed I was either too tall or too thin for my age," he recalls. "I was always getting into fights because of my size." He was most comfortable on the sand soccer fields near his home, where the rugged competition fueled his burning desire to win.

"I always hated to lose at soccer," he says. "I would do anything to help my team win. Sometimes, I would get mad at the other people on my team if I saw they were not trying as hard as they could."

Hakeem often played soccer on this sand playground across from his house (visible in the background). The crooked metal poles and crossbar form the only goal on the field.

Winning at soccer, not basketball, dominated his thoughts as he was growing up. "I was not planning on a basketball career," Hakeem says. "Basketball was just something I did because I enjoyed it. You see, as a young boy I grew tall very fast. All my friends told me I should leave soccer and try basketball. They said my body was suited to the sport." His friends had a point. The slender Hakeem had grown to a height of 6 feet, 9 inches by the time he was 16.

Hakeem was born January 21, 1963, the third of six children in his family. His father, Salaam, and mother, Abike, ran a successful cement business in Lagos, the capital of and largest city in Nigeria. As a small boy growing up with his four brothers and one sister, Hakeem dreamed of traveling to the United States to attend college. He hoped to become a scholar.

"Students in Nigeria are always told about the fine colleges and universities in the United States," Hakeem says. "It always was my desire to get good grades in high school so that someday I could attend college in America." Athletics were not in his dream. He did see himself squeezing in an occasional game of team handball or soccer after class, but not until his mid-teens did he discover basketball.

Hakeem's parents, Salaam (left) and Abike (right), sold cement from a storage shed attached to their house.

Olajuwon says he was spotted by Richard Mills, coach of the Nigerian national junior basketball team. "He called me over," Hakeem says, "and right away he impressed upon me the value of playing basketball and eventually joining the Nigerian juniors." Olajuwon told Mills his primary goal in life was to go to college in the United States. "Richard Mills was certain that I could achieve my goal through basketball."

Mills arranged for Olajuwon to join the Lagos state junior basketball team. Nigeria is divided into 19 states, and the city of Lagos is a state in itself. Each state has its own junior basketball team.

Among the coaches for Olajuwon's new team were two Nigerian basketball legends, Kamu Otemibaggbe and Sunny Basket (whose given name is Sunday Osagiede). Hakeem credits both coaches with helping him to polish his skills on the basketball court. "The three of us worked long and hard," Hakeem says. "I still remember how helpful it was for me to spend hours and hours going one-on-one with Sunny Basket."

Hakeem was an instant success playing for the Lagos junior team, which won a gold medal at the Nigerian National Sports Festival. From there, the team traveled to Angola to participate in a tournament of teams from central Africa. That's where Olajuwon met Christopher Pond, the man who would eventually help him accomplish his dream of attending college in the United States.

Christopher Pond (left) first saw Hakeem play basketball in Africa. Later, Christopher dropped in on Hakeem (center), who by then was a standout college player and had begun what would become a long relationship with Lita Spencer (right).

Raised in the United States, Pond was coaching basketball in Africa through a sports exchange program. He was impressed when he saw Hakeem playing, especially when he learned that Hakeem was a soccer player who had played basketball for only a short time. Pond thought Olajuwon had some shortcomings, but he was sure the tall teenager would improve with coaching and practice. He had never seen an African player with so much raw potential for basketball.

The two talked, then both went their separate ways. A short time later, Hakeem was one of two players selected from Lagos to participate on the Nigerian national team. "I met with Oliver Johnson, the national coach of the Nigerian men's basketball team," says Hakeem. "He accepted me to play for the men's team, even though I was not ready then. He wanted me to practice, play with these men."

Olajuwon was only 17, but Johnson soon had him scrimmaging with Olympic athletes who were an average of 25 years old. "They were grown men," he says, "and I was a growing boy. What an experience!"

As overwhelmed as he was to play for the national senior team, he was more awed by what happened next. Pond had arranged for him to go to America. "He said he had been contacting many United States college coaches about me," Olajuwon said. Several coaches agreed to give him a tryout. "Christopher Pond," Hakeem says, "made it all possible for me."

On October 10, 1980, Olajuwon boarded a plane bound for the United States. His first stop was to be St. John's University in Jamaica, New York, where he was scheduled to try out for the school's team, the Redmen. When the plane landed at John F. Kennedy Airport in New York City, Hakeem gathered his carry-on baggage, moved to the door, and stepped onto the ramp leading from the plane to the terminal. There, he received a major shock.

A brutal, numbing sensation shot through his body. The temperature outside was freezing cold!

The United States was not supposed to be like this, he thought. "It was just too cold," Olajuwon says. "Right away, I had the feeling I could not survive in America. The weather was too different from Lagos." Temperatures in the southern part of Nigeria usually range from 65°F to 87°F throughout the year.

Had the weather been more agreeable in New York, Hakeem might have played at St. John's University.

"The windchill that day in New York must have been zero," says Hakeem. "I was in shock." To make matters worse, he had brought along only lightweight, warm-weather clothes.

Immediately, Hakeem sought out the nearest airline agent and showed her his ticket. She told him that his next destination, Houston, Texas, would be warmer. "I told her I wanted to go to Houston NOW! I didn't want to go to St. John's University." She made the ticketing change, and Olajuwon was on the next flight to Texas.

Houston's warm, humid weather was a welcome relief, but Hakeem didn't get a warm reception there.

The University of Houston campus, pictured against the Houston skyline

No one met him at the airport, so he had to hire a taxi to drive him to the University of Houston. When he arrived at basketball practice, Hakeem found that coach Guy Lewis wasn't expecting much from him.

"Look," says Lewis, "I've had hundreds of foreign kids referred to us over the years. Frankly, they just don't play basketball in most countries the same way we play it in the U.S." Lewis told Hakeem to sit on the bench and watch the varsity scrimmage.

"I had heard so much about the skills of the American players," Hakeem says. "Now I was watching them play in person. I must admit it was different than I had thought. You see, I thought they would be perfect. I didn't expect them to ever miss the basket. What a surprise it was for me when they did!"

Olajuwon soon realized these were mere mortals he was watching, not supermen. "I did observe," he says, "that they were much taller than the competition I was used to in Nigeria. I wanted the coach to put me in the game right away to see if I could compete with these men."

Finally, Lewis sent him into the scrimmage. Hakeem remembers that he was "calm and confident. I found I could play with them as an equal."

Coach Lewis, however, remembers differently. He thought the soft-spoken Olajuwon was "too much of a gentleman" under the boards and that his 190-pound body wasn't strong enough to withstand the rough play. Nevertheless, Lewis saw enough potential to invite Hakeem back.

Eighteen-year-old Hakeem was soon offered a scholarship to play for the University of Houston Cougars. Unfortunately, he had arrived too late to attend fall-semester classes. He enrolled in spring classes, planning a major in business technology. In the weeks before the spring semester began, Hakeem easily completed the university's foreign student entrance requirements. English wasn't a problem for him. Like many Nigerians, Hakeem speaks more than one language. He is fluent in four Nigerian languages, French, and English (which, because Nigeria was once ruled by Great Britain, is the country's official language).

During his first summer in Houston, under orders from Coach Lewis, Hakeem embarked on a program to gain weight. He quickly adapted to a high-calorie diet.

Rice, yams, okra, soups, sauces, and fruits are typical Nigerian foods. Nigerian tradition dictates that food is eaten only to sustain the body. "Back home," Hakeem said, "I would eat a bowl of rice and maybe a small piece of chicken for lunch." At Houston his lunch would usually begin with five pieces of chicken. Hakeem also enjoyed Texas barbecue and, especially, vanilla ice cream. Almost before he knew it, he had gained 50 pounds.

Hakeem was surprised at how little the people he met knew about Nigeria. "People think all of Africa is the jungle because that's what they see on TV. But Lagos is just like New York—crowded, people walking 24 hours a day," he said.

Throughout the summer of 1981, Hakeem was constantly playing basketball at Houston's Fonde Recreation Center. There he met some top players from the NBA. Olajuwon competed against Houston Rockets players Robert Reid, Allen Leavell, and Moses Malone.

Lagos is a very crowded, busy city.

Moses Malone, who played for the Houston Rockets from 1976 to 1982, was named Most Valuable Player of the NBA three times—in 1979, 1982, and 1983.

The 6-foot, 10-inch Malone became Hakeem's hero. A dominant NBA center, Moses had averaged 27.8 points, blocked 150 shots, and had hauled down 1,180 rebounds in the 1980–81 season. At 27 years old, he was in peak form, and the inexperienced Olajuwon was no match for him. "In our one-on-one games, Moses would beat me and beat me," Hakeem says.

Yet something about Olajuwon impressed Malone. The young man's agility, honed on the soccer fields of Africa, allowed him to make an unusually high number of steals for a big player. Malone saw a lot of himself in Olajuwon, and he vowed to help the young player succeed not only in college basketball but in the professional game as well.

Day after day, Moses showed Hakeem how to use his elbows and shoulders to box out opponents. The more he jostled under the backboards with Moses, the more Hakeem found himself enjoying the action. Moses taught Hakeem how to position himself for rebounds and demonstrated many of his offensive moves. He helped Hakeem learn to concentrate all through the game.

"He always had lots of talent," Moses recalls, "but we had to work him hard to keep his mind in the game." Spending the summer in Houston at the Fonde Recreation Center would pay off for Hakeem.

Phi Slama Jama

3

Olajuwon began his first college season, 1981-82, on the bench. Despite Hakeem's hard work with Malone and the other pros over the summer, Coach Lewis thought his new player lacked the "court sense" to be a starter.

Olajuwon was disappointed, especially since he had perfected a new shot that he felt was unstoppable. "It was a jump hook," he says. "Moses did it on me. I liked it, so I asked him to do it again so I could watch and learn." He practiced the shot over and over, until he knew he could make it consistently.

Hakeem thought his jump hook would be a deadly weapon against defenders, but the shot failed to impress Lewis. "He still didn't know how to post up [position himself under the basket] properly," says Lewis. "He had no power move to the basket. Sure, he could jump, but he didn't know where and when."

During the 1981–82 season, there was little indication that Hakeem Olajuwon was on his way to greatness. Hakeem's statistics for his first year of college basketball were average. In 29 games, he scored 8.3 points and had 6.2 rebounds per game. He missed four games after suffering back spasms.

Even though his numbers were not spectacular, Olajuwon had gradually gained the confidence of Coach Lewis. The coach put Hakeem into the starting lineup six times toward the end of the season. This came as the team was headed to a 25-8 record and the National Collegiate Athletic Association (NCAA) Tournament. The Cougars made it all the way to the NCAA Final Four before losing to the eventual champion, the University of North Carolina, 68-63.

During the summer of 1982, Hakeem returned to the Fonde Recreation Center for more one-on-one sessions with Moses Malone. Now a full 7 feet tall and 245 pounds, Olajuwon refused to be bullied by Malone under the boards, or anywhere else. The pros at the recreation center hardly recognized him. "He's ready [to dominate games]," Malone said early that summer. "He's got aggressiveness, talent, strength, youth, and he can jump out of the building."

Another endorsement came from Coach Lewis. "I've told Hakeem that he will be a starter this season—until he shows that he's not one," Lewis told Houston sportswriters.

The Cougars, including Hakeem, were successful playing under the hard-nosed Coach Lewis (left).

Outside of Houston, Hakeem had barely been noticed — until the Cougars reached the Final Four in 1982. But during the 1982–83 season, he grabbed the spotlight. Fans recognized him by his nickname — Hakeem the Dream. Playing in all 34 University of Houston games, Hakeem led the nation in shots blocked, rejecting 175 of his opponents' efforts. He averaged 13.9 points per game and grabbed 388 rebounds. He also led the Cougars back to the NCAA Final Four.

Houston beat Louisville, 94-81, in its first Final Four matchup, then lost to North Carolina State, 54-52, in a heartbreaking championship game. Olajuwon had 20 points in the loss, and he was named Most Valuable Player in both the Midwest Regional Tournament and the Final Four. It was the first time in 17 years that the Final Four MVP Award had been given to a player from a losing team. In five NCAA Tournament games, Hakeem averaged 18.8 points per game, had 32 blocked shots, and shot 66 percent from the field.

"Suddenly, he is the most towering, if not the most terrifying player in college basketball," columnist Dave Anderson wrote in the *New York Times.*

What really gained the attention of the nation's media was Olajuwon's 68 dunk shots that season.

Left: Hakeem listened to music as he practiced for Houston's game against Louisville in the 1983 Final Four. Right: Sports fans were impressed by Hakeem's ability to "play above the rim."

"Whirling, spinning, backboard-quivering dunks," *People* magazine called them.

Hakeem and his teammates had become known as the "Phi Slama Jama" fraternity, a nickname given to them by *Houston Post* columnist Thomas Bonk. Joining Olajuwon in the mythical fraternity were starters Clyde Drexler, Larry Micheaux, Michael Young, and Alvin Franklin.

In spite of his role in the team's success, Hakeem didn't let it affect his approach to life. A follower of the Islamic religion since his childhood, he remained a devout Muslim. (The Muslim holy book is the Koran, which is the source of Islamic law and ritual. Its words are considered to be those of God—called *Allah* by Muslims—spoken to the messenger Muhammad by an angel.)

At the core of Muslim life is the family, and Hakeem never forgot his parents, brothers, and sister. He would telephone home twice a week, usually at midnight (which is 6:00 A.M. in Lagos).

Often he would tell his mother about his success on the basketball court, but she paid little attention. "She always wanted to know about classes and how I was doing as a university student in America. To my parents, education came first. They wanted me to return with a business law degree."

Hakeem often felt that his father wanted him to return to Lagos someday and take over the family cement business. As much as he respected his parents, Hakeem knew he wouldn't fulfill their wishes. Deep down inside, he knew that basketball, not cement, would be his future.

Even though he enjoyed his life in the United States, Hakeem often missed his family, his friends, and the customs and food of Africa. No one in all of Nigeria made *fufu*—a dish made from pounded yams—like Hakeem's mother. Hakeem dreamed of someday making enough money to bring his family, and all the *fufu* they could carry, to the United States.

The University of Houston Cougars began the 1983–84 season without veterans Clyde Drexler and Larry Micheaux from the 1983 national runners-up. Micheaux had graduated, and Drexler left school early for the NBA. Before long, though, Coach Lewis had found the right combination of players to replace their talent. After losing the first game, Houston ran off a string of 10 straight victories.

The Cougars opened their Southwest Conference schedule in January 1984 with a 10-2 non-conference record. "Even with all the young players we have," said starting forward Michael Young, "I think we have matured. I feel good about the rest of the season."

If Young and the Cougars felt good, the rest of the Southwest Conference teams soon learned they had plenty of cause for concern. Houston reeled off 15 conference victories in a row before losing the final regular-season game. The team finished the season with a record of 26-4, and Olajuwon led the nation in three categories: field-goal percentage (67.5), shots blocked (207), and rebounding (500). He became only the third player in NCAA Division I history to lead in two or more categories for the same season. He was also named first-team All-America by the major reporting services, but the honors were secondary to his goal of winning a national championship for Houston.

Coach Lewis gives the Cougar players instructions during a time-out in Southwest Conference Tournament action.

Houston warmed up for the 1984 NCAA Tournament by winning the Southwest Conference Tournament. Then the Cougars began their quest for the national championship. Twice before, Olajuwon and the Cougars had advanced to the Final Four, and twice they had been denied. They were determined that they would not be three-time losers.

Houston had little trouble getting back to the Final Four. The Cougars beat Louisiana Tech, Memphis State, and Wake Forest in the early rounds of the NCAA Tournament. Houston's next obstacle to the championship was the University of Virginia. With two seconds remaining in overtime, Houston led, 49-47. Virginia guard Othell Wilson drove into the foul lane, fully intending to sink the shot that would send the game into a second overtime. Seemingly coming from out of nowhere, Hakeem easily swatted away Wilson's shot, and the ball bounced harmlessly off to the side. Once again, Houston had qualified for the national championship game.

The Cougars had little time to celebrate the Virginia win. Up next were the Georgetown Hoyas and their highly regarded center, Patrick Ewing, in the finals at the Seattle Kingdome. "I really want to play against Patrick Ewing," Hakeem said, "not to prove whether I am better, but because I want to play against the best."

Unfortunately, the battle of the greatest college centers failed to live up to its billing. At halftime Olajuwon was in foul trouble, and Georgetown led, 40-30. Hakeem picked up his fourth foul just 23 seconds into the second half. Even with Hakeem playing more cautiously, Houston cut the Hoya lead to four points before Georgetown pulled away for good. The Hoyas won, 84-75.

Neither center had an outstanding game. They both led their teams with nine rebounds, but neither led in scoring. Hakeem had 15 points to Ewing's 10.

Although he was upset with some of the officials' calls, Hakeem held his feelings back and congratulated the Hoyas. He was young. He would have other chances for a championship, he reasoned. The only difference would be that the honor would have to be obtained in the professional, not collegiate, ranks. He had decided to skip his final college season and declare himself eligible for the NBA draft.

Hakeem was all smiles as he told reporters that he would join the NBA in the fall of 1984.

In the last two seasons, he had started every Cougar game at center, and his team had won 63 games while losing only 8. His team had gone to the Final Four each year he was on the squad. College basketball's loss would be professional basketball's gain.

At 7 feet, 4 inches, Ralph Sampson (left, in white uniform) teamed with 7-footer Hakeem Olajuwon (number 34) to terrorize opponents under the basket. The two were Houston's Twin Towers for three seasons.

Twin Towers

4

While the Houston Cougars were among the best teams in college, the crosstown Houston Rockets were one of the worst teams in the NBA. Moses Malone had left the Rockets for Philadelphia before the 1982-83 season began. Teamed with Julius "Dr. J" Erving and Andrew Toney, Malone continued his success and helped the 76ers win the 1983 NBA championship. In the meantime, the Rockets suffered in his absence. Never a standout franchise, Houston had posted only three winning seasons since the team was formed in 1967.

In 1983-84, for the second season in a row, Houston had posted the worst win-loss record (29-53) in the Western Conference. At the time, the last-place finisher in each conference participated in a coin flip to decide which team would pick first in the college draft. The year before, the Rockets had won the coin flip and had selected 7-foot, 4-inch University of Virginia All-American Ralph Sampson.

The Rockets won the coin flip again in 1984. This time, the team selected Olajuwon. Hakeem would stay in Houston, not as a Cougar but as a Rocket. Head coach Bill Fitch immediately announced that Sampson and Olajuwon would be his "Twin Towers" for years to come.

Hakeem enjoyed instant success in his rookie NBA season. On October 27, 1984, in his first regular-season NBA game, he led the Rockets with 27 points, as Houston posted a 121-111 road victory over the Dallas Mavericks.

"He's got great physical skills, quickness, and move-ment, and he has a wonderful attitude," said Pete Newell, a former coach at the college and Olympic levels who had worked with Olajuwon that summer. "He just needs more experience and to understand what his mistakes are. He'll be an excellent NBA player." Newell knew what he was talking about. After retiring from coaching college teams, Newell ran clinics and camps to help centers and forwards develop their skills.

On December 6, 1984, in a loss to the Golden State Warriors, the Rocket rookie broke loose and scored 42 points. "This is fun," Hakeem said after the game. "In college, the other teams would hang all over me with their zone defenses. Here I have more room to do what I want with the basketball. I find this to be very enjoyable."

A lineup featuring Sampson and Olajuwon was a potent weapon for the Rockets. The pair became the first twosome since Wilt Chamberlain and Elgin Baylor of the 1970 Los Angeles Lakers to average 20 points and 10 rebounds for a season. Sampson, Rookie of the Year at the center position the year before, was happy to yield the spot to Olajuwon. Even though he was four inches taller than Hakeem, he felt more comfortable playing a forward position.

At least one of his opponents, Moses Malone of the Philadelphia 76ers, was familiar to Hakeem during his rookie season.

Hakeem liked Bill Fitch's coaching style.

On the basketball court, Hakeem felt more at ease than ever before. His new coach, Bill Fitch, used humor and gentle prodding to get his points across, rather than yelling at his players as Coach Lewis had.

Former University of Houston teammate Clyde Drexler, who had joined the Portland Trailblazers, said, "Hakeem knows what's expected of him in the NBA, and he'll go out and do it, because not to do it would be a cause for embarrassment. He doesn't want to be embarrassed. He wants to go first-class all the way."

Hakeem attracted all kinds of attention from sports-writers and basketball fans across the country. Despite his success and fame, there were times he was treated like a regular rookie.

One day, Hakeem was a few minutes late for practice, so the impish Fitch played a prank on him: He told Hakeem he was trading him to the Cleveland Cavaliers in Ohio. Olajuwon was crushed. He didn't understand that he had become yet another victim of typical Fitch humor until sympathetic teammates let him in on the gag. Later, when Houston traveled to a cold, snowy Cleveland, Hakeem fully understood Fitch's joke. "Then I knew why the coach picked Cleveland for my new home," Olajuwon laughed.

The 1984–85 Rockets made a dramatic turnaround from previous years' performances. Houston placed second in the NBA Midwest Division with a 48-34 record. Not surprisingly, Sampson and Olajuwon finished one-two in team scoring. Ralph averaged 22.1 points per game and Hakeem 20.6. Olajuwon snared 974 rebounds and blocked 220 shots. Sampson had 853 rebounds and 168 blocks.

Hakeem finished fourth in the league for rebounding, and second for blocked shots. He was second in the Rookie-of-the-Year balloting. The winner that year was Chicago Bulls guard Michael Jordan.

Once again, Hakeem was part of a team that was in the hunt for a championship. The Rockets had easily qualified for the NBA play-offs. Once again, though, Hakeem was denied a championship. The Rockets lost in the first round when the Utah Jazz won the five-game series, three games to two.

By the time Hakeem's second professional season began, he was an established veteran, earning the respect of his teammates, NBA coaches, and opponents. "I don't believe anybody thought there would be a player quite like Hakeem," said Rockets general manager Ray Patterson, "because there was no experience to suggest it. It's like people didn't think there would be a 16-foot pole-vaulter or a four-minute miler. People just didn't know there would be someone with that combination of strength, size, and quickness at the center position."

Hakeem earned respect as a strong, quick center.

Hakeem hits the floor and attempts to reach a loose ball ahead of Magic Johnson during Houston's play-off series with Los Angeles.

In addition to the Twin Towers, the 1985–86 Houston Rockets featured forward Rodney McCray and guards John Lucas and Lewis Lloyd. Robert Reid, Allen Leavell, Jim Petersen, and Mitchell Wiggins provided bench strength. The Rockets had to overcome the late-season loss of Lucas, the point guard, who was suspended after he tested positive for drug use. Then guard Allen Leavell suffered a season-ending injury.

Olajuwon led the team in scoring for 39 out of 82 regular-season games. He had a season-high 41 points against Portland on November 5, and scored in double figures every game of the season. Propelled by Olajuwon's 23.5 points and 11.5 rebounds per game, and Sampson's 18.9 points and 11.1 rebounds per game, Houston finished the regular season with 51 wins—a new team record.

This year, there would be no repeat of 1985's disappointing play-off performance. The Rockets swept Sacramento in three games to open the postseason, then defeated Denver, four games to two, in the second round.

The next opponent, however, was tougher. Houston was up against the defending NBA champion Los Angeles Lakers for the Western Conference Championship.

The two teams traded victories on the Lakers' home floor to start the series. Then they moved to The Summit in Houston, where Olajuwon outscored Kareem Abdul-Jabbar, 40-33, in game three to lead the Rockets to victory. Two nights later, Hakeem again led all scorers, and the Rockets won game four. They led the series, three games to one, and needed to win just one more game.

In game five, Olajuwon was ejected late in the fourth quarter—along with the Lakers' Mitch Kupchak —for fighting. With just seconds remaining in the game, the score was tied, 112-112. The Lakers ran the clock down and tried to score just before time ran out. Laker guard Byron Scott missed a long jumper, however, and the Rockets rebounded. Houston called a time-out immediately. With one second showing on the clock, the game appeared to be headed into overtime.

Sampson took the inbounds pass about 10 feet from the basket, turned, and shot the ball quickly. It struck the rim and bounced in. Just like that, Houston had won the series. The Rockets had qualified for the championship series!

The long NBA season was drawing to a close, with Houston and the Boston Celtics matched in the NBA Finals—a best-of-seven-games series. The first two games were to be held at Boston Garden, where 15 NBA championship banners already hung from the ceiling.

Shortly after Houston took a 65-64 lead in the third quarter of game one, Olajuwon picked up his fourth and fifth fouls in the space of 32 seconds. Coach Fitch said afterward: "We were in it, then Hakeem picked up his fifth foul. Then, within a period of 30 seconds, we turned the ball over three times." Boston took advantage of the mistakes to post a 112-100 victory.

Things didn't improve for the Rockets in game two. Led by Larry Bird, Boston won again, 117-95. "Bird is the greatest player I have ever seen," Hakeem told reporters after the game. "He will shoot the ball from anywhere, and there is nothing you can do about it."

Hakeem took a brief rest during practice the week Houston played Boston for the NBA championship.

Rockets Jim Petersen (left) and Hakeem Olajuwon (right) battle Boston's Bill Walton (center) for control of a missed shot at the Houston net.

The series moved to Houston and the friendlier surroundings of The Summit. "We will have more confidence when we play in our own building," Olajuwon promised. "There is no way they can beat us in Houston."

Hakeem made believers of the hometown crowd. The Rockets, who trailed by eight points with three minutes left in the game, came back. Houston out-scored Boston by 10 points in the final minutes to win the game, 106-104.

Even though they had great support from the home fans, the Rockets lost game four, 106-103. They were behind in the series, three games to one. Houston had to win in game five, or the series—and the Rockets' hopes for a championship—would end.

As it turned out, Houston won, although no one could have predicted the turn of events. Ralph Sampson was ejected from the game in the first half for punching Boston's Larry Sichting and starting a bench-clearing brawl. Despite losing Sampson, Houston had built a 25-point lead by the middle of the fourth quarter. The Rockets won easily, 111-96. Olajuwon led the way with 32 points, 14 rebounds, 3 assists, and 2 steals. He also blocked 8 Boston shots.

The series returned to Boston Garden for game six, and Larry Bird put the finishing touches on yet another Celtic championship. He had a triple-double with 29 points, 11 rebounds, and 12 assists as Boston coasted to a 114-97 win.

For Hakeem, the outcome was the same. He had come so close to a championship, but the other team had spoiled his dream. "They had the best team." he said in the Boston Garden locker room. "We didn't do it. They played great. We tried our best. The game just didn't go the way we wanted it to."

Hakeem spends time at home with his daughter, Alon, during one of her visits. Alon's mother is Lita Spencer, Hakeem's former girlfriend.

5

Home

On the outskirts of southwest Houston, near a private lake, is Hakeem's house—a one-story, white stucco, two-bedroom home with arched windows and a flat roof. "I wanted my house to be casual but elegant," Hakeem said. "This house is part of my heritage, part of the Islamic culture. You can look at my house and sense that the owner is a Muslim. The house has meaning behind it."

Partly as a concession to Hakeem's height, the ceilings are 16 feet high. Plenty of windows and open space allow Hakeem to display his art collection to great effect. "One of the main things I wanted to achieve," he said, "is a sense of openness for my art work." Collecting abstract art has become one of his passions.

Another passion is clothing fashion. He is one of the best-dressed players in the NBA. "I could discuss fashion for hours and hours," he says. "Dressing is like a piece of art. You have to put the combinations together. You have to know true quality."

Every summer, Hakeem's parents journey to Houston to visit. They stay at the townhouse that Hakeem bought and lived in before his house was built. Hakeem also remains close to the rest of his family. He stays in touch with his older brother, Adeyemi Kaka, and sister, Kudi, who still live in Lagos. His younger brothers, Akin, Taju, and Afis, followed Hakeem to the United States to pursue their education.

GQ magazine, also known as Gentleman's Quarterly, named Hakeem to its "NBA All-Star Style Team" for his fashion sense. Skybox issued a special trading card to recognize the honor.

Hakeem's brothers, Taju (left) and Afis, played basketball together for the University of Texas at San Antonio during the 1991–92 season. Afis still plays for the Roadrunners.

When Taju was a senior (during the 1991–92 season), he and Afis, then a sophomore, played basketball together at the University of Texas at San Antonio. Neither brother is as tall as or as talented at basketball as Hakeem, but they manage to give Hakeem some stiff competition when the three square off in pickup games. "It gets pretty intense when we play against each other," Afis said. "When he makes a dunk on us, he reminds us of it all day. But if we beat him, you know we let him know it."

Hakeem has a daughter, Alon, who was born in 1988. She lives with her mother, Lita, but visits

Hakeem regularly. "She's wonderful," he said. "She's what life is all about."

Hakeem uses his house and his family as a retreat from his celebrity status. "I want to be treated as a human being, not a special person. Don't look at me as being special because I am a tall adult who plays basketball for a living. I know some people talk and react differently when they think I am a celebrity, and I don't enjoy that. I feel uncomfortable. People must realize that I am a person just like them.

"If you respect me as a man, then I, in turn, will respect you."

Hakeem remains close to his family—those who live in Lagos as well as his brothers in the United States. Some of his relatives are (back row, left to right): brother-in-law Dipe, sister-in-law Elizabeth, sister Kudi, brother Afis, brother Adeyemi, mother Abike, father Salaam, and brother Taju. The young children in front are Hakeem's nephew and niece. (The photograph is from 1983, taken in front of the Olajuwons' home in Lagos.)

After the 1985–86 season, many basketball observers were picking Hakeem to succeed the aging Abdul-Jabbar as the NBA's top center. "Hakeem's at the top right now," said Portland's Clyde Drexler. "He produces more than any center in the whole league. The numbers don't lie." Olajuwon averaged 23.5 points per game—slightly more than Abdul-Jabbar—and 11.5 rebounds per game—many more than Abdul-Jabbar. Olajuwon also blocked 3.4 shots per game, compared to Abdul-Jabbar's 1.6.

Street and Smith's Pro Basketball said of him: "He has the offensive capabilities of a younger Abdul-Jabbar, the rebounding tenacity of Moses Malone, and runs the floor better than Robert Parish. As if that weren't enough, he has the fearlessness and the desire to make the big play—late in the game, the mark of the truly great ones."

With Hakeem developing into a dominant player, most observers thought Houston would repeat as Western Conference champions in 1986–87. Instead, the team sagged to a 42-40 record—third in the Midwest Division standings.

One reason for the downslide was Sampson's frequent injuries. He played in only 43 games and would never be injury-free again during his NBA career. Sampson faded rapidly the next season, and the Rockets traded him to Golden State. The Twin Towers had become the Lone Tower in the Lone Star State.

For the second year in a row, Olajuwon was named to the All-NBA first team, but the Rockets couldn't get past the first round of the play-offs.

Even so, Olajuwon demonstrated his abilities. Against Dallas in the 1987–88 play-offs, he set an NBA record for a four-game series by scoring 150 points. He had 41 points and 26 rebounds in the third game of the series and 40 points and 15 rebounds in the fourth game.

"He's a thoroughbred," said Fitch. "When you jump on his back, he'll carry you." But Hakeem could carry his coach only so far. When the team continued to lose, the Rockets fired Fitch and replaced him with Don Chaney.

Hakeem's fifth professional season, 1988–89, was one of his best. He led the NBA with 13.5 rebounds per game and averaged 24.8 points. He also had 3.4 blocked shots and 2.6 steals per game. He was the first player in NBA history to get more than 200 steals and 200 blocked shots in the same season. He was named to the All-NBA first team for the third straight year.

"Some people say I improved," he said, "but I really don't look at it that way. There wasn't anything I did last year that I couldn't do two years ago. I think if our team gets better, that's how I'll be able to take my game to a higher level. If we become more balanced as a team, I will be able to help the other players, and they will be able to help me."

That year, Olajuwon became outspoken with his thoughts about youth and education. He disliked seeing young athletes spending so much time playing basketball and so little time studying. "Everyone wants to play in the NBA," he said, "but very few will make it. Education is the key to success. It is much more important to learn how to express yourself, to communicate with others and share your experiences."

In the 1989-90 season, Hakeem led the NBA in rebounding for the second consecutive season, with 14 per game. He also led the league in blocked shots with 4.6 per game.

Hakeem was off to a good start again in 1990-91, but then he suffered a major injury two months into the season. On January 3, 1991, Olajuwon and Chicago Bulls center Bill Cartwright were battling for a rebound. Cartwright's elbow caught Hakeem in the eye, sending him to the floor in pain. Doctors diagnosed the injury as a "blowout" fracture of the right orbit, which is the bone structure that holds the eye.

Hakeem went on the disabled list and missed the longest stretch of games in his career. He underwent surgery on January 14, and doctors proclaimed the operation a success. Olajuwon returned to the lineup on February 28, wearing protective goggles.

Houston was 16-13 before Hakeem's injury, and went on to win the game against Chicago the night he was hurt. The team went 15-10 without Hakeem, then finished 20-7 with him back in the lineup. At 52-30 for the season, Houston had posted the best record of its 24-year history. The Rockets entered the play-offs, but lost in the first round for the fourth consecutive season.

Hakeem surprised many people in the basketball world in March 1991 by telling reporters—who had been writing *Akeem* for 10 years—that from then on he would be spelling his first name *Hakeem*. He said

Hakeem is actually the correct Arabic spelling of the name, but the pronunciation was the same as always. In Arabic, Hakeem means "wise one" or "doctor."

When Hakeem returned to action following his eye injury, he wore goggles to avoid reinjuring the eye.

The next season, Olajuwon was optimistic because of the team's success the year before, especially when he was sidelined. "I do not have to be the one scoring all of the points and making all of the plays anymore," he said. "For several years, I have felt that way and maybe some people have wondered why. But it was just a matter of the team that I had around me. The team is now much better."

Hakeem gets frustrated when the Rockets lose.

Surrounding Hakeem in the starting lineup were NBA standouts Otis Thorpe, Eric "Sleepy" Floyd, Kenny Smith, and Buck Johnson. Yet somehow the chemistry so essential for creating a winning unit just wasn't there. The great season that Hakeem anticipated never materialized. He missed several games when he was hospitalized with an irregular heartbeat, and later when he was sidelined with a pulled hamstring muscle. Coach Don Chaney was fired midway through the season, and longtime assistant coach Rudy Tomjanovich was named as his replacement. The team failed to make the play-offs.

As the season closed, Hakeem was discouraged. He even said he didn't want to play for the Rockets anymore. Houston fans worried that Rockets management might finally trade their star center. Several times during his career, Hakeem had openly disagreed with team management, criticized teammates, asked for a new contract, and demanded to be traded.

As the 1992-93 season began, though, Hakeem was back in his Rockets uniform, leading Houston to a string of early victories. "Sometimes people don't understand me," he told reporters. "I think a lot of you don't understand how much I want to win. What I want to do in the years I have left in basketball is the only thing I have not yet achieved.

"I want to win a championship."

HAKEEM OLAJUWON'S BASKETBALL STATISTICS

University of Houston Cougars

Year	Games	Points	PPG	Rebounds	RPG	Blocks	Steals
81–82	29	240	8.3	179	6.2	72	26
82–83	34	472	13.9	388	11.4	175	47
83–84	37	620	16.8	500	13.5	207	61
Totals	100	1,332	13.3	1,067	10.7	454	134

College Highlights:

NCAA Tournament MVP, 1983.
All-America, 1984.

Houston Rockets — Regular Season

Year	Games	Points	PPG	Rebounds	RPG	Blocks	Steals
84–85	82	1,692	20.6	974	11.9	220	99
85–86	68	1,597	23.5	781	11.5	231	134
86–87	75	1,755	23.4	858	11.4	254	140
87–88	79	1,805	22.8	959	12.1	214	162
88–89	82	2,034	24.8	1,105	13.5	282	213
89–90	82	1,995	24.3	1,149	14.0	376	174
90–91	56	1,187	21.2	770	13.8	221	121
91–92	70	1,510	21.6	845	12.1	304	127
Totals	594	13,575	22.9	7,441	12.5	2,102	1,170

Career Highlights:

All-Star game, 1985, 1986, 1987, 1988, 1989, 1990, 1992, 1993.
First team All-NBA, 1987, 1988, 1989.
Second team All-NBA, 1986, 1990.
Third team All-NBA, 1991.
First team All-Defensive, 1987, 1988, 1989.
Second team All-Defensive, 1985, 1991.
All-Rookie Team, 1985.

ACKNOWLEDGMENTS

Photographs are reproduced with the permission of: pp. 1, 2, 6, 59, 63, John Biever; pp. 9, 22, Houston Rockets; p. 10, Milwaukee Bucks; pp. 12, 13, 54, William Campbell/*Sports Illustrated;* p. 15, Manny Millan/*Sports Illustrated;* p. 17, St. John's University; pp. 18, 24, 27, 29, 32, 41, University of Houston; p. 21, CIDA Photo/Bruce Paton; pp. 28, 34, 39, 44, 47, 48, The Bettmann Archives; pp. 36, 40, 50, Bill Baptist; pp. 43, 60, Brian Drake; p. 52, George R. Rekela; p. 53 (both), John Poindexter/University of Texas at San Antonio; and pp. 56, 64, Bill Gillingham.

Front cover photograph by John Biever. Back cover photograph by Brian Drake.